ISBN-13: 978-0692632710
ISBN-10: 0692632719

Raptors are birds that hunt and feed on other animals. They are also known as **"birds of prey."**

The name "raptor" come from the Latin word **"rapere"** which means to seize or capture.

All raptors are **carnivores** (meat eaters). Different raptors have different diets. They might eat mammals, reptiles, fish, birds, insects, amphibians, shellfish, worms or insects. There is also a species of vulture that eats palm fruit: The palm fruit vulture.

Raptors have been admired and even worshipped in many cultures around the world. Raptors have also been exploited and killed in the name of decoration, sport, ritual and protection of livestock.

All raptors are protected by law in the United States and it is illegal to possess any part of a raptor, even a feather.

The study of birds is called **ornithology**, and there are 446 species of raptors.

Birds of prey have great eyesight that they use for hunting. Vision is the raptors most important sense. Raptors can even perceive the color range of ultraviolet which humans cannot.

Birds in general have the largest eyes for their size in the animal kingdom and are very similar to that of a reptile eye. Owls have eyes that are 2.2 times bigger than that of birds of the same weight.
Each eye has two eyelids and a transparent, moveable membrane for protection.

Raptors have sharp, curved talons which they use for grabbing and holding their food. Most raptors have very strong feet for this purpose. However, most "New- world" vultures have comparably weak feet.

Many raptor species are used in the sport of "falconry." Falconry is the hunting of wild game using a trained bird of prey in their natural habitat.

The footgear above is called a "**jess**." It's made of leather and is used in falconry to keep control of the bird when it's on the handler's glove.

Raptors have strong, sharp, hooked beaks used for tearing and ripping flesh from their prey. Raptors have a small triangular tooth called a **"tomila"** in the upper beak. It is used to quickly kill its prey by cutting the spinal cord.

Red-Tailed Hawk

Raptors hunt live prey or they will scavenge from animals that have already died, known as "**carrion**." Many raptors are important to the environment by acting as a "clean-up crew."

This cape buffalo has been stripped clean by vultures.

These turkey vultures and black vultures make quick work of an animal carcass.

Bald eagle

Many Raptors are considered "apex predators."
This means they are at the top of the food chain and
do not have any natural enemies.

Golden eagle

A **"species"** is a group of organisms that are similar and can breed and produce fertile offspring.

Animals that are active during the day, such as eagles, are called **"Diurnal."**

Animals, like owls, that are active at night are called **"Nocturnal."**

Names like "Red-Tailed hawk" and "Bald Eagle" are known as **"common names."** Animals of different species can share the same common name.

Scientists talk about animals using their **"Scientific name."** Every species of animal on earth has its own unique scientific name. This helps scientists make sure they are talking about the same animal.

Scientific names are always in Latin and are often difficult to read and pronounce, but they are very important. So it's fun to try! Give it a shot! The scientific name for humans is *(Homo sapien)* which in Latin means "wise person."

Every raptor in this book will have its common name AND its scientific name,
because NATURE KIDS LOVE SCIENCE!!

SPECIES

Osprey

Falco haliaeetus

Wingspan: 127 – 180 cm (50 – 71 in)

Ospreys are unique as they are in a group all to themselves. Ospreys and owls are the only raptors whose outer toe is reversible. This means they have two in front and two behind which makes it easier for them to grasp slippery fish. Ospreys are found worldwide and are the second most widespread raptor after the peregrine falcon.

Ospreys breed near freshwater rivers and lakes, they build nests out of sticks on high structures like cliffs, poles and trees. Whenever you are near water and see a breeding platform, chances are that it has been built for ospreys.

Hawks

There are 226 species of hawks.

Hawks can see 8 times better than humans.
Hawks are able to see different colors, unlike many
other animals.
Hawks can dive as fast as 150 miles per hour!
Most hawks build nests in trees using twigs and branches.
"**Buzzard**" is a name for some species of large
hawks that eat carrion.

Pale chanting goshawk

Red-tailed hawk

Ferruginous hawk

Red-Tailed Hawk
Buteo jamaicensis
Wingspan: 110 - 145 cm (43 - 57 in)

Red-Tailed Hawks are large birds with a very distinctive red tail.

Red-Tailed Hawks are probably the most common hawk in North America.

They are often seen on telephone poles or soaring in circles high in the air hunting for prey on the ground.

Whenever you hear the screech of a bird of prey on TV or in the movies, it's almost always a Red-Tailed Hawk, not an eagle as we are often led to believe.

Harris Hawk
(Parabuteo unicinctus)

Wingspan: 130 - 120 cm (41 - 47 in)

Harris Hawks live in the Southwestern United States, Chili and Argentina. These raptors are very intelligent, social and hunt in packs of two to six. Their thick skinned legs allow them to perch on cactus.

Swainson's Hawk
(Buteo swainsoni)

Wingspan: 117 - 130 cm (46 - 54 in)

Inhabiting mainly North America, they are also called the grasshopper or locust hawk.

They will fly low over the ground, run or hover while they hunt mainly for insects, but when they are feeding their chicks they will provide the three Rs: rodents, rabbits and reptiles. When they are breeding they are very aggressive, chasing off intruders like red-tailed hawks, golden eagles and turkey vultures.

They will also flock in the thousands when it's time to migrate south.

Northern Harrier
(Circus cyaneus)
Wingspan: 97 – 122 cm (38 – 48 in)

Northern Harriers live in the northern parts of the Northern Hemisphere in North America and Eurasia.

Males perform elaborate flying barrel roles to impress females.

Northern Harriers have a "face disc" that resembles

that of an owl.
They fly low over the ground when hunting; weaving back and forth. They hunt small mammals and birds, but they will also take larger animals by drowning them. Each male may mate with several females at the same time and they build their nests on the ground.

Black-Chested Buzzard-Eagle
(Buteo melanoleucus)

Wingspan: 149 - 200 cm (4 ft 11 in - 6 ft 7 in)

This huge "eagle-like" buzzard which is actually a type of hawk, lives in open regions of South America. They eat carrion, birds, snakes, lizards and mammals like the European rabbit which now lives in its range. This is helpful to farmers as the rabbits can eat crops and become pests.
Its call sounds like *kukukukuku.*

Eagles

There are over 60 species of eagles in the world.

Eagles are large and powerfully built. Most eagles are larger than most all other birds of prey except for some vultures.

Eagles build their nests on cliffs or in tall trees. Many species lay only two eggs. When the chicks hatch the larger chick will often kill the smaller one so that it gets all the food and has a better chance of survival.

The remaining chick is usually a female as they are bigger than the males.

When an eagle talon strikes its prey, the force is twice as strong as a bullet.

Eagles have about 7000 feathers.

Bald eagle
(Haliaeetus leucocephalus)

Wingspan: 1.8-2.3 m (5.9-7.5 ft)
Latin for "sea eagle" and "white head."

Ranging throughout North America, Bald Eagles eat mostly fish, but will also eat carrion. Bald Eagles can swoop down at 100 mph to grab their prey. They can carry the heaviest load of any bird; 15 pounds!
The National bird of the United States, they were put on the endangered species list in 1967 and have since grown in numbers.
Bald eagles build VERY large nests, the largest of any bird, sometimes weighing as much as one ton (2000 pounds)!
Bald eagles start life being completely brown with only a few white streaks, they develop white feathers on their head and tail as they mature.

Golden eagle
(Aquila chrysaetos)

Wingspan 1.8 - 2.34 m (5 ft 11 in - 7 ft 8 in)

A very large bird which, in the past, has been used for hunting gray wolves!

The Golden Eagle is extremely powerful and is North America's largest raptor. It is the National symbol of Mexico.

They eat rodents, reptiles, fish, rabbits, birds and can even kill an adult deer!

Harpy Eagle
(Harpia harpyja)
Wingspan 5'9"- 7'4"

Harpy Eagles are the largest and most powerful raptor found in the Americas. They live in Mexico, Central America and parts of South America.
They hunt mainly for mammals that live in trees such as monkeys and sloths.
They have even been known to kill lambs, goats, pigs and even deer!

Kites

There are 22 known species of kites in the world.

Red kite

There are five species of kites in North America.

- Swallow-tailed kite
- Mississippi kite
- Snail kite
- Hook-billed kite
- White-tailed kite

Kites are found on all continents except for Antarctica.

Kites get their name from their ability to soar on wind currents as they hunt for prey.

Swallow-Tailed Kite
(Elanoides forficatus)

Wingspan: 1.12 – 1.36 m (3.7 – 4.5 ft)

These cool looking raptors are the largest of all the kites. They eat dragonflies and small reptiles such as lizards and snakes, and will often eat their prey while flying. The Swallow-Tailed Kite ranges from the southeastern United States to Peru. Their numbers are threatened by habit destruction and are considered endangered by the state of South Carolina.
Their call sounds like *kwi-kwi-kwi-kwi.*

Red Kite
(Milvus milvus)
Wingspan: 175 – 179 cm (69 – 70 in)

This beautiful raptor lives in Western Europe and Northwestern Africa. It feeds on birds, small mammals such as mice, voles and rabbits as well as carrion like sheep carcasses.
Red kites will often decorate their nests with plastic, paper and other random man-made items.

Brahminy Kite
Haliastur indus
Wingspan: 109 - 124 cm (3.6 - 4.1 ft)

The Brahminy Kite is an ocean loving scavenger and hunter that lives in India, Australia and Southeast Asia.

They love fish, insects and small mammals. They will also group together and mob other raptors to steal their food.

They build their nests near water, in trees, out of sticks, seaweed and driftwood.
Immature birds will play by dropping leaves and catching them in mid-air.

Falcons

There are more than 40 different species of falcons.

Falcons are known for their speed and incredible flying ability. They have tapered wings which allow them to change direction very quickly.

Falcons are found all over the world in every continent.
Five species of falcons live in the United States.

- Peregrine falcon
- Merlin
- American kestrel
- Prairie falcon
- Gyrafalcon

Gyrafalcon

Merlin

Peregrine Falcon
(*Falco peregrinus*)

Wingspan: 74 - 120 cm (29 – 47 in)

The Peregrine Falcon is the fastest member of the animal kingdom reaching speeds of 200 miles per hour during its high speed dive! It is the world's most widespread raptor, it's found just about everywhere except polar regions, rainforests and high mountains. Their call sounds like kek-kek-kek.

Peregrine Falcons hunt mostly other birds such as pigeons, ducks and song birds. They will even hunt other smaller raptors!
Prey is swooped upon and grabbed right in mid-air!

Gyrafalcon
(Falco rusticolus)
Wingspan:110 - 130 cm (43 - 51 in)

The gyrafalcon is the largest falcon species. They live and breed mostly in the Arctic regions and the northern islands of North America, Europe and Asia.

They hunt ground birds like grouse as well as mammals such as voles and rabbits. Gyrafalcon's feathers change color from brown to white based on the region in which they live. It was a highly valued hunting bird with the Vikings and is the National symbol of Iceland.

Red-Footed Falcon
(*Falco vespertinus*)
Wingspan: 65 – 75 cm (26 – 30 in)

These small falcons live in Eastern Europe, Asia and winters in Africa. In 2004 one was even found on an island off of Massachusetts! They eat insects, rodents, reptiles, amphibians and birds. These cool little raptors are heavily threatened due to habit destruction.

Crested Caracara
Caracara cheriway

Wingspan:
107 – 130 cm (42 – 51 in)

The Crested Caracara is a cool looking raptor which looks "falcon-like" but acts like a buzzard. Caracaras live mainly in Mexico, Central and South America. Caracaras have long legs and like to stay near the ground. As scavengers, they feed mainly on carrion but will also feed on easily caught mammals, insects, reptiles, amphibians and shellfish.

Caracaras compete for food with vultures. and dominate the carcass' they find.
They are often called Mexican eagles, even though they are not eagles at all.

Owls
There are over 150 species of Owls in the world.

There are 19 species of Owls in North America.
Owls are nocturnal.
Owls have eyes on the front of their faces like humans.

Many have ears that are located on different parts of their
head to give them superior hearing.
Many Owls have a "facial disc" that funnels sound to
their ears. The hearing is magnified as much as 10 times,
which is far greater than that of humans.

Owls have two toes that face forward and two that face
backwards to give them a more powerful grip.
Owls can turn their heads 270 degrees.
After eating, Owls **regurgitate** (throw up) the bones,
feathers and fur of their prey that couldn't be digested.
These chunks are called owl pellets.

Eurasian eagle Owl

(Bubo bubo)

Wingspan: 188 cm (6 ft 2 in)

The Eurasian Eagle Owl is one of the largest owls in the world. Similar in size to a golden eagle. They are heavy bodied with tall ear-tufts and feathered talons. They have cool pumpkin to blood-orange colored eyes.

Eurasian Eagle owls mainly live in mountains and forests of Europe and Asia.
This nocturnal predator hunts for mammals, birds, fish, invertebrates and even other owls.
They will take their prey on the ground or in full flight.
They live about 20 years in the wild but have been know to live more than 60 years in captivity.
Eurasian Eagle Owls are apex predators and the real threats to them come from traffic collisions, poisoning, electrocution and shooting.

Snowy Owl
(*Bubo scandiacus*)
Wingspan: 125 – 150 cm (49 – 59 in)

The Snowy Owl is native to Arctic regions of North America and Eurasia.
They are large raptors with yellow eyes and black beaks.

Males are almost all white while the females have a greater number of gray feathers. Snowy Owls nest on the ground by building on top of mounds or boulders with a good view for hunting. Males may mate with two females at

once about a kilometer apart. When chicks are born there can be a big difference in their sizes, but they do not kill their smaller nest mates like some eagles do.
Their nests can be raided by Arctic foxes, wolves and predatory birds.
Snowy Owls eat mainly lemmings and other small rodents as well as larger mammals such as squirrels, rabbits and even raccoons!

Barn Owl
(*Tyto alba*)
Wingspan: 80 - 95 cm (31 - 37 in)

Barn Owls live in more places then any other owl. They hunt at night for mice, voles and rats. They fly very quietly and their feathers are very soft. The feathers are not very waterproof, so they get wet when it rains.

Farmers try to attract barn owls as they can eat over 1,200 mice a year!

Vultures

There are 16 species of **"Old World"** vultures which are found in Africa, Asia and Europe.

There are 7 species of **"New World"** vultures that live in the Americas. They are related to storks and herons.

Vultures are scavengers that eat carrion.

Vultures have bald heads to keep themselves clean of blood and meat from their food and to keep cool.

Vultures have super strong stomach acid to kill the bacteria from near spoiled corpses.
Vultures will regurgitate their food; sometimes to flee from predators or to keep predators away from their nests.

Vultures have a keen sense of smell, which is among the best in the animal kingdom.

Vultures are super smart and trainable.

Vultures are important as they keep the environment clean of dead animals and prevent the spread of disease.

Griffon vulture

(Gyps fulvus)

Wingspan: 2.3 – 2.8 m (7.5 – 9.2 ft)

The Griffon Vulture is a very large, heavy bodied, Old World vulture that lives in Eurasia and was once numerous in many Eurasian countries.

Its population has been heavily reduced and eliminated altogether in some places due to hunting and poisonous baits. Countries such as Italy and France have reintroduced the raptors and hopefully their numbers will grow in the future.

In 2003 a woman was hiking in the Pyrenees Mountains. She fell off a cliff to her death where vultures consumed her body leaving only her clothes and bones.

Egyptian Vulture
(Neophron percnopterus)

Wingspan: 155 - 170 cm (5.1 - 5.6 ft)

Egyptian Vultures are Old World vultures that can be found in Southwestern Europe, Africa and India.

Egyptian Vultures are the smallest of all vultures and will eat carrion, mammals, birds, reptiles, rotten fruits, rotten vegetables and the eggs of other birds.

They will pick up pebbles and use them as tools to break open the shells. The use of tools is quite rare in birds.

Egyptian Vultures are also known for eating poop, including human poop. The poop has pigments that give them their yellow and orange skin.

White-Headed Vulture
(*Trigonoceps occipitalis*)
Wingspan: 207 – 230 cm (7 - 7.5 ft)

The White-Headed Vulture is an Old World vulture
from Africa.

They eat carrion, flamingoes, small mammals
and lizards.

White-Headed Vultures are critically endangered and
are disappearing at an incredibly fast rate. They are
being killed by poisoning, hunting, lack of food and
changes in their environment by humans. Farmers
unintentionally poison them when they lay bait for
jackals and other predators. Poachers poison them so
that they do not draw attention to their illegal activities.

Bearded Vulture
(*Gypaetus barbatus*)
Wingspan: 2.31 – 2.83 m (7.6 – 9.3 ft)

Bearded Vultures are considered Old World vultures that are sparsely populated throughout mountainous regions of Europe, Asia and Africa.

They live where predators like golden eagles and wolves are common and their leftover kills can be eaten. They usually don't eat the meat. Instead they eat bone marrow. Sometimes they will attack live tortoises as prey, grab them, fly high, then drop them to crack open their shell.

The Bearded Vulture is different in that it does not have a bald head, instead, it is feathered with black on its throat which is where its name comes from.

King Vulture
(*Sarcoramphus papa*)
Wingspan: 1.2 – 2 m (4 – 6.6 ft)

King Vultures are colorful New World vultures found in Central and South America. They live in tropical forests, savannas and grasslands.
They are masters of conserving their energy.

When flying, they will often soar for hours without getting tired. The King Vulture does not have a voice box, any noises it does make are croaks and wheezes. They will eat cattle carcasses, lizards, fish and injured animals.

King Vultures nest on the ground and only lay a single egg. Both parents care for the chick and regurgitate food to feed it.

California Condor
(Gymnogyps californianus)
Wingspan: 3.0 - 3.05 m (9.8 -10 ft)

The largest American land bird, the California Condor
is a New World vulture that came to the brink of
extinction due to poisoning,
poaching and habitat destruction.

In 1997 there were only 27 of these condors left in the
world. A conservation and reproduction effort began
and in 1991 condors began to be reintroduced into the
wild. California Condors are one of the rarest bird
species. In 2014 there were 425 condors living in
Arizona, Utah and California.
The California Condor's neck will change color based
on its emotional state. This is believed to be used in
communication with one another.
Native Americans used condor feathers and bones for
headdresses, decoration and rituals.

Turkey Vulture
(*Cathartes aura*)
Wingspan: 160 – 183 cm (5.5 - 6 ft)

Turkey Vultures live all throughout South America, the United States and up to Southern Canada. It is the most widespread New World vulture.

Turkey Vultures eat mostly carrion and can smell the gasses produced from rotting corpses.

The name "Turkey Vulture" comes from its head's similarity to that of a turkey. They gather into large groups to roost and hop clumsily as they walk with their weak feet.

Turkey Vultures can be attacked by great-horned owls, red-tailed hawks, eagles, raccoons and foxes. In the United States many people refer to turkey vultures as "buzzards" even though they are not true buzzards.

Made in the USA
Las Vegas, NV
21 June 2021